J Ref 959.704 Vie
Vietnam War. Reference library
cumulative index /

CYF $5.00

HARRIS COUNTY PUBLIC LIBRARY

3 4028 04632 5040

D0887434

Vietnam War
Reference Library
Cumulative Index

Vietnam War
Reference Library
Cumulative Index

Cumulates Indexes For:

Vietnam War: Almanac
Vietnam War: Biographies
Vietnam: Primary Sources

Gerda Raffaelle,
Index Coordinator

AN IMPRINT OF THE GALE GROUP

DETROIT · SAN FRANCISCO · LONDON
BOSTON · WOODBRIDGE, CT

Vietnam War Reference Library: Cumulative Index

Gerda Raffaelle, *Index Coordinator*

This publication is a creative work copyrighted by U•X•L and fully protected by all applicable copyright laws, as well as by misappropriation, trade secret, unfair competition, and other applicable laws. The authors and editors of this work have added value to the underlying factual material herein through one or more of the following: unique and original selection, coordination, expression, arrangement, and classification of the information. All rights to this publication will be vigorously defended.

Copyright © 2001

U•X•L, An Imprint of The Gale Group

All rights reserved, including the right of reproduction in whole or in part in any form.

ISBN: 0-7876-5576-7

Printed in the United States of America

10 9 8 7 6 5 4 3 2 1

Cumulative Index

A = Vietnam War: Almanac
B = Vietnam War: Biographies
PS = Vietnam War: Primary Sources

A

Abrams, Creighton W.
A 127 (ill.), 128
B *2:* 434-35, 435 (ill.), 436
Academy Award
B *2:* 363, 403, 404
Acheson, Dean
A 127
After the War Was Over: Hanoi and Saigon
B *2:* 387
African Americans in the U.S. military
PS 25-27
African Americans in the U.S. military, discrimination against
PS 26-27
Agent Orange
A 184, 191 (ill.)
B *2:* 284-85
Agnew, Spiro
B *1:* **1-6**, 1 (ill.), *2:* 329
PS 109, 131
Agroville Plan
A 57

Aiken, George
A 140
Alcatraz
PS 181
Ali, Muhammad
A 140
PS 38-39
Alvarez, Everett, Jr.
PS 181
Amerasian Homecoming Act
A 261
Amerasian Immigration Act
A 261
Amerasians
A 261
American Friends Service Committee
PS 171
American soldiers. *See also* Vietnam veterans
American soldiers, and atrocities
A 152-53, 169-70
B *1:* 32-36
PS 151-53, 157-58, 163
American soldiers, and Vietnam
A 157-74, 219-22

Boldface type indicates abbreviation of individual titles.

Italic numerals indicate volume.

Bold numerals indicate main biographical entries.

Illustrations are marked by (ill.).

1

American soldiers, background of
A 159-63
American soldiers, combat
experiences of
A 163-67, 164, 166 (ill.), 219-22
B *1:* 129; *2:* 282-83, 334,
376-77, 401-2, 415
American soldiers, decline
in morale
A 170-73, 219-22
American soldiers, drug use
A 171-72, 220
American soldiers, emotional
bonds among
PS 150-51
American soldiers, emotions of
A 168
American soldiers, experiences
in Vietnam
PS 114-15, 147-63, 149 (ill.),
153 (ill.), 162 (ill.)
American soldiers, experiences
of women among
PS 165, 177
American soldiers, racial
tensions among
A 173, 220
PS 25-27, 40-41
American soldiers, relations with
Vietnamese people
A 167-70, 220
B *1:* 89
PS 114, 150
American soldiers, severity of
injuries sustained in combat
PS 166-68
Americanization
A 91-92
Andreotta, Glenn
B *1:* 34
Antiwar movement
A 105-11, 106 (ill.), 123, 126,
129, 133-55, 149 (ill.), 151
(ill.), 185, 207-9, 211, 225
B *1:* 4, 19-21, 39-40, 41, 55-57,
159; *2:* 283, 326, 328,
373, 374
PS 12, 21, 23 (ill.), 24, 29, 79,
80, 81, 83-84, 86, 92, 93,
96, 97 (ill.)
Antiwar movement, and
military draft
PS 61-67, 64 (ill.), 66 (ill.)

Antiwar movement, and Vietnam
veterans
A 152-53, 179-80
Antiwar movement, March on
the Pentagon
A 140-41
B *1:* 143-44
Antiwar movement, Moratorium
Day demonstrations
A 145, 207
B *1:* 57
PS 80
Antiwar movement, on
college campuses
A 138-39, 146-47
Antiwar movement,
problems within
A 142-43
B *1:* 145-46
Antiwar movement, protests at
1968 Democratic
Convention in Chicago
A 129, 143-45
B *1:* 45, 47-51, 55-56, 119,
144-45, 155; *2:* 326
PS 79
Antiwar movement, reaction to
Kent State University killings
PS 108-9
Antiwar movement, teach-ins
A 139
Antiwar veterans
A 152-53
B *1:* 199-200
Ap Bac, Battle of
A 64-65
B *1:* 116
Apocalypse Now
B *1:* 131; *2:* 343
*Argument without End: In
Search of Answers to
the Vietnam Tragedy*
B *2:* 280
Army of the Republic of Vietnam
(ARVN)
A 43, 54, 63, 66
PS 134-35, 136-37, 138-44, 145
Army of the Republic of Vietnam
(ARVN), performance of
A 65, 98-99, 224, 226, 243,
245, 248
Arnett, Peter
A 137
PS 121 (ill.)

Arrogance of Power, The
    B *1:* 103
ARVN. *See* Army of the Republic
    of Vietnam (ARVN)
As I Saw It
    B *2:* 374
Atrocities
Attrition. *See* United States,
    strategy of attrition
    PS 151-53, 157-58, 163
August Revolution
    B *1:* 137
    PS 5

B

Bad War, The
    B *2:* 284
Baez, Joan
    B *1:* **7-14**, 7 (ill.), 96
Ball, George
    A 136-37, 137 (ill.)
Ban Me Thuot
    A 244-45
Bao Dai
    A 13 (ill.), 14, 18, 25, 29, 39, 43
    B *2:* 289, 290, 298, 300
Barry, Jan
    A 153
Battle for Hue. *See* Hue, Battle for
"Battle Hymn of
    Lieutenant Calley"
    B *1:* 35
Battle of Ap Bac. *See* Ap Bac,
    Battle of
Battle of Dien Bien Phu. *See* Dien
    Bien Phu, Battle of
Battle of Ia Drang. *See* Ia Drang,
    Battle of
*Before the Revolution: The
    Vietnamese Peasants under
    the French*
    A 16-17
Berrigan, Daniel
    B *1:* **15-23**, 15 (ill.)
Berrigan, Daniel, and Catonsville
    Nine
    B *1:* 20-21
Berrigan, Philip
    B *1:* **15-23**, 15 (ill.), 18, 19, 20-
    21, 41
Best and the Brightest, The
    B *1:* 117

Bigart, Homer
    A 53
Black Panther Party
    B *1:* 122
Boat people. *See* Vietnamese
    refugees
Body count
    B *1:* 32
    PS 124-25
Bonaparte, Napoleon III
    A 8
Born on the Fourth of July (book)
    B *1:* 196, 200
Born on the Fourth of July (film)
    B *1:* 196, 201-2; *2:* 400, 403-4
Brezhnev, Leonid
    B *2:* 330
*Bright Shining Lie: John Paul Vann
    and America in Vietnam, A*
    B *2:* 382, 386-87
Brother Nhu. *See* Ngo Dinh Nhu
    (Brother Nhu)
Brown, Sam
    A 145
Briarpatch, the
    PS 181
Buddhist protests
    PS 45
Buddhist suicides
    A 67-69, 68 (ill.)
    B *2:* 293, 299-300, 301
Buddhist uprisings
    A 61, 67, 69-70
    B *2:* 293-94, 308
Bui Diem
    PS 46
Bundy, McGeorge
    B *1:* **24-29**, 24 (ill.); *2:* 239, 371
Bunker, Ellsworth
    B *2:* 250, 306
Burdick, Eugene
    B *2:* 207
Bush, George
    A 287, 287 (ill.), 288-89, 291
Byrne Jr., Matthew
    B *1:* 71

C

CALCAV. *See* Clergy and Laity
    Concerned About Vietnam
Calley, William
    A 212-13, 213 (ill.)

B *1:* **30-37**, 30 (ill.)
  PS 152-53, 163
Cambodia
  A 205 (map), 233, 252 (ill.),
    253 (ill.), 266-68, 270-72
  B *2:* 243, 244-45, 247, 359-68,
    389-95
Cambodia, seizure by Khmer
    Rouge
  A 253-54
Cambodia, U.S. bombing of
  A 205-6
  PS 82
Cambodia, U.S. incursion into
  A 209-12
  B *2:* 328
Cambodia, U.S. invasion of
  B *2:* 328
  PS 91-92, 95-96, 109
Campaign for a Landmine
    Free World
  B *2:* 287
Can Lao Party
  B *2:* 300
Canada
  B *2:* 355
  PS 64-65, 69
Canterbury, Robert
  PS 100
Caputo, Philip
  A 98, 163, 164, 282
  PS 114, 151, 153, 154-55,
    156-61
Carmichael, Stokely
  A 142
  PS 28, 28 (ill.)
Carter, Jimmy
  A 279
  PS 75
Case, Clifford
  A 140
Case-Church Amendment
  A 239
  B *2:* 329
  PS 131
Catholic Peace Fellowship
  B *1:* 19
Catonsville Nine
  B *1:* 18, 20-21
Central Intelligence Agency
    (CIA). *See* U.S. Central
    Intelligence Agency (CIA)
  A 40
  PS 84

Chicago Eight
  B *1:* 56, 119, 123, 145
Chicago Seven
  A 144-45
Child of War, Woman of Peace
  B *2:* 228-29
  PS 146
China
  A 1, 3, 4-5, 6, 29-30
  B *2:* 330
Chinese Exclusion Act of 1882
  PS 218
Christmas Bombing
  A 217, 231-32
  B *1:* 192; *2:* 220
CIA. *See* U.S. Central Intelligence
    Agency (CIA)
Civil Rights, Bill of 1964
  A 82
Civil Rights Memorial
  B *2:* 235
Civil rights movement
  A 140
  PS 29
Civilian relief workers
  PS 114, 166, 170
Clark, Ramsey
  B *1:* **38-44**, 38 (ill.)
Clark, Tom
  B *1:* 38, 39
Clay, Cassius.
  PS *See* Ali, Muhammad
Clergy and Laity Concerned
    About Vietnam (CALCAV)
  A 138
  B *1:* 15, 186
  PS 29
Clifford, Clark
  A 126-27
Clinton, Bill
  A 272, 289, 291-92
  PS 195
Coffin, William Sloan
  B *1:* 40
Colburn, Lawrence
  B *1:* 34
Colby, William
  A 44, 66
  B *2:* 208 (ill.)
Cold War
  A 25-27, 46
  B *2:* 324
  PS 9

Collins, J. Lawton
B *2:* 299
Collins, Joseph L.
A 45
Colonialism
A 7
Coming Home
B *1:* 96, 201
Commission on Campus Unrest
PS 102-3
Committee of National
Reconciliation
B *2:* 321
Communism
A 27-29, 47
Con Son prison
B *2:* 211, 216, 347
PS 183
Confucianism
A 4
Confucius
A 4-5, 5 (ill.)
Conscientious Objectors
A 150
PS 39, 63-64
Containment doctrine
A 27
Counterinsurgency techniques
B *2:* 208
Convoy of Tears
A 245-48
Cronkite, Walter
A 123
PS 114, 120-21, 124-25, 127,
127 (ill.), 129, 131
Cruise, Tom
B *1:* 202
Cu Loc Prison. *See* Zoo, the
Cuban Missile Crisis
B *1:* 170-71; *2:* 371

D

Da Nang
A 247
B *2:* 251
Daley, Richard J.
A 144
B *1:* 45-51, 45 (ill.), 125
Daley, Richard M.
B *1:* 51
Davis, Rennie
B *1:* 55

De Behaine, Pigneau
A 8
Dear John letters
PS 152
Death and Life of Dith Pran, The
A 8
B *2:* 365
Dellinger, David
A 144
B *1:* 52-57, 52 (ill.), 123
Democratic Kampuchea.
See Cambodia
Democratic Party
PS 49
Democratic Presidential
Convention. *See* Antiwar
movement, protests at 1968
Democratic Convention
in Chicago
Democratic Republic of Vietnam.
See North Vietnam
Denton, Jeremiah
B *1:* 58-63, 58 (ill.)
PS 181, 184, 192
*Derailed in Uncle Ho's
Victory Garden*
B *2:* 344
Dewey, A. Peter
A 26
Dien Bien Phu, Battle of
A 32-35, 33 (ill.), 116
B *2:* 421, 424-25
Dispatches
A 124
B *1:* 127, 129, 130-31;
2: 339, 343
Dith Pran
B *2:* 362-63, 364-65, 365 (ill.)
Dogs in the U.S. military
A 160-61, 161 (ill.)
Doi moi economic reforms
A 268-70
B *2:* 350
Doi Quan Toc Dai
(Long-Haired Army)
B *2:* 314
Domino Theory
A 27, 28, 34
Doubek, Bob
B *2:* 378
Douglas, Helen Gahagan
B *2:* 325
Doves
A 136

Draft, North Vietnamese
  PS 65
Draft, U.S. military
  A 150, 158-59
  B 2: 333
  PS 59-68, 74-75, 176-77
Draft, U.S. military, and methods
    of avoiding
  A 158-59
  PS 59-67
Draft, U.S. military, resisters of
  PS 39, 65-66
Dulles, John Foster
  A 45
Duong Van Minh (Big Minh)
  A 72, 73, 248
  B 2: 294, 301, 305, 318-19
Durbrow, Eldridge
  A 45

E

Eagleton, Tom
  B 2: 270
East Meets West Foundation
  B 2: 228
  PS 146
Easter Offensive
  A 148, 217, 227-30, 243
  B 2: 426
Economic Research and Action
    Project (ERAP)
  B 1: 121
Eisenhower, Dwight D.
  A 28, 34, 42, 46-47, 47 (ill.), 48
  B 1: 108; 2: 238, 325, 407, 408
Elbring, Judy
  B 1: 76
Ellsberg, Daniel
  A 225
  B 1: 64-72, 64 (ill.); 2: 385
Ellsberg, Daniel, and
    Pentagon Papers
  B 1: 64, 67-71
ERAP. See Economic Research and
    Action Project (ERAP)
Evans, Diane Carlson
  B 1: 73-78, 73 (ill.)

F

Faas, Horst
  B 2: 345

Faith of My Fathers
  B 2: 263
Fall, Bernard
  B 1: 79-86
FBI. See Federal Bureau of
    Investigation (FBI)
Federal Bureau of
    Investigation (FBI)
  PS 83-84
Fellowship of Reconciliation
    (FOR)
  A 136
Filo, John
  PS 110
Fire in the Lake: The Vietnamese
    and Americans in Vietnam
  B 1: 87, 89-91
First Indochina War
  A 23-25, 29-35, 46, 54
  B 2: 212, 347, 421
  PS 8
First Indochina War, U.S. aid to
    France during
  A 31-32
FitzGerald, Frances
  B 1: 87-91, 87 (ill.)
Flynn, Sean
  B 2: 345
Fonda, Jane
  B 1: 92-97, 92 (ill.), 126
Fonda, Jane, and POWs
  B 1: 95-96
Food for Peace Program
  B 2: 267
FOR. See Fellowship of
    Reconciliation (FOR)
Ford, Gerald
  A 151, 241, 241 (ill.), 246, 247
  B 1: 193-94; 2: 251, 252 (ill.),
    253, 329, 330
  PS 227
Ford Motor Company
  B 2: 273
Forrestal, accident on board
  B 2: 259
Forsythe, Julie
  PS 114, 165-77
Fragging
  A 172
  PS 41
France
  A 1, 23, 24-25, 32, 38
  PS 4

France, colonialism in
    Southeast Asia
    A 9 (map)
France, colonialism in Vietnam
    A 8-12, 19-20
    B *2:* 289
Free-fire zones
    B *1:* 32
*From Yale to Jail: The Life Story
    of a Moral Dissenter*
    B *1:* 57
Front for National Salvation
    B *2:* 300
Fulbright, William
    A 86, 105, 136
    B *1:* **98-104**, 98 (ill.)
Full Metal Jacket
    B *1:* 131, 132 (ill.)
Fuller, Jack
    A 286

G

Galbraith, John Kenneth
    A 63
Garwood, Robert
    PS 196
Geneva Conventions
    PS 179, 180, 183
Geneva Peace Accords
    A 34, 37, 39, 40, 42, 44
    B *2:* 347
    PS 1, 8-9, 14
Gibbs, Phillip
    PS 111
Going after Cacciato
    B *2:* 332, 335
Goldwater, Barry
    A 81, 88, 88 (ill.)
    B *1:* **105-12**, 105 (ill.), 153;
        2: 262
Goldwater, Barry, and
        1964 election
    B *1:* 108-10
Goodacre, Glenna
    B *1:* 76
    PS 232
Gorbachev, Mikhail
    A 271
Green, James
    PS 111
Greene, Graham
    A 54-55, 55 (ill.)
    B *2:* 207

Gruening, Ernest
    A 86
Guerilla warfare
    A 100
    B *2:* 431
Gulf of Tonkin incident
    A 75, 82-85

H

Hagel, Chuck
    PS 232 (ill.)
Haig, Alexander
    B *1:* 5
Halberstam, David
    A 53, 67, 109, 137
    B *1:* **113-18**, 113 (ill.); *2:* 403
    PS 131, 140, 140 (ill.)
Haldeman, H. R.
    B *1:* 4
Hanoi Hilton
    B *2:* 259-60
    PS 181
Harkins, Paul
    A 53
Harris, David
    B *1:* 13
    PS 67
Hart, Frederick
    B *2:* 234
    PS 223
Hatfield, Mark
    A 140
    B *2:* 269
Hawks
    A 136
Hayden, Tom
    A 144
    B *1:* 55, 94, 96, 97, **119-26**,
        119 (ill.)
Hayslip, Le Ly
    PS 114, 133-46
Heaven and Earth
    B *2:* 229, 404-5
    PS 146
Hell in a Very Small Place
    B *1:* 83
Herr, Michael
    A 124
    B *1:* **127-33**; *2:* 339, 343
Hersh, Seymour
    A 212
Heschel, Abraham
    B *1:* 19

Hiss, Alger
  B *2:* 324
Hitler, Adolf
  B *2:* 308
Hmong people of Laos
  PS 212-13
Ho
  B *1:* 117
Ho Chi Minh
  A 12, 13, 15-16, 17, 18 (ill.),
    18-19, 20, 24, 28, 29, 37-39,
    41, 42, 43, 44, 96, 118, 136
  B *1:* 55, 84, **134-40,** 134 (ill.),
    137 (ill.); *2:* 210, 211, 212,
    213, 216, 290, 307, 312, 346,
    349, 422, 423
  PS 1, 2, 3-20, 17 (ill.),134, 191
Ho Chi Minh, Communist
    beliefs of
  PS 16
Ho Chi Minh, death of
  A 206-7
Ho Chi Minh, nationalist
    feelings of
  PS 16
Ho Chi Minh City. *See* Saigon
Ho Chi Minh Trail
  A 49-50, 100, 205, 274
  B *2:* 392, 398
Hoa Lo Prison. *See* Hanoi Hilton
Hoffa, James
  B *1:* 176
Hoffman, Abbie
  A 144
  B *1:* 123, **141-47,** 141 (ill.)
Hoffman, Abbie, and Yippies
  B *1:* 144-46
Hoffman, Julius
  B *1:* 123, 145
Holbrooke, Richard
  PS 131
Home before Morning: The Story of
    an Army Nurse in Vietnam
  B *2:* 413, 419
Hoover, J. Edgar
  B *1:* 40
  PS 110
House Un-American Activities
    Committee (HUAC)
  B *2:* 324
HUAC. *See* House Un-American
    Activities Committee (HUAC)
Hue, Battle for
  A 121-22

Hue massacre
  A 246
Humanitas
  B *1:* 14
Humphrey, Hubert H.
  A 129, 129 (ill.), 130, 144, 145
  B *1:* 3, 41, 50, 154-55, 155 (ill.),
    179; *2:* 268, 291
  PS 54, 95, 121-22
Hun Sen
  A 267
  B *2:* 247, 367, 394-95
Hussein, Saddam
  A 287, 288
  B *1:* 42
Huynh Cong "Nick" Ut
  B *2:* 354, 355, 357

I

Ia Drang, Battle of
  A 99
ICBL. *See* International Campaign
    to Ban Landmines (ICBL)
ICP. *See* Indochinese Communist
    Party (ICP)
If I Die in a Combat Zone, Box Me
    Up and Ship Me Home
  B *2:* 335
In Love and War
  PS 115, 185-90
In Retrospect: The Tragedy and
    Lessons of Vietnam
  B *2:* 275, 276-77, 278-80
In the Combat Zone: An Oral
    History of American Women
    in Vietnam
  PS 114
In the Lake of the Woods
  B 332, 337
Indochina Peace Campaign (IPC)
  B *1:* 96, 126
Indochina War. *See* First
    Indochina War
Indochinese Communist
    Party (ICP)
  A 13
  B *1:* 136; *2:* 210, 211, 216,
    312, 347
Indochinese Union
  A 9
Institute for the Study of
    Nonviolence
  B *1:* 12

International Campaign to Ban
  Landmines (ICBL)
  B *2:* 281, 286-87
IPC. *See* Indochina Peace
  Campaign (IPC)
Iran hostage crisis
  A 282-83

J

Jackson State College
  A 211
  PS 111
Japan, occupation of Vietnam
  A 14-15
JCS. *See* Joint Chiefs of Staff (JCS)
JFK
  B *2:* 404
Joffe, Roland
  B *2:* 362
Johnson, Lyndon B.
  A 75, 76, 77-78, 79 (ill.), 81-82,
    84, 85-88, 87 (ill.), 89, 94,
    96-97, 104, 105, 111, 113-14,
    117-18, 126-28, 138, 140,
    141, 143, 225
  B *1:* 27-28, 39, 40, 41, **148-64**,
    148 (ill.), 152 (ill.), 173,
    177-79, 184-86; *2:* 241, 268,
    275, 277, 278, 308, 319,
    326, 371, 373, 406, 410, 411,
    430, 432, 433-34
  PS 18, 48-49, 53-54, 63, 85
Johnson, Lyndon B., and advisors
  known as "Wise Men"
  A 127
  B *2:* 242, 411-12
Johnson, Lyndon B., and J.
  William Fulbright
  B *1:* 101-3
Johnson, Lyndon B., and 1964
  election
  B *1:* 108-10
  Johnson, Lyndon B., and Tet
    Offensive
  PS 126-27
Johnson, Lyndon B., as vice
  president
  B *1:* 151-52
Johnson, Lyndon B., decision not
  to seek reelection
  A 127-28, 144
  B *1:* 161, 162-63

Johnson, Lyndon B., decision to
  increase U.S. military
  involvement in Vietnam
  A 89
Johnson, Lyndon B., Great
  Society programs
  A 77-78, 81-82, 104
  B *1:* 156, 160
Johnson, Lyndon B., Vietnam
  War policies of
  B *1:* 70-71, 157-63
Johnson, Jr., Sam Ealy
  B *1:* 149
Joint Chiefs of Staff (JCS)
  B *2:* 406, 409, 429, 435, 436
Joint Relief International
  Denton Operations
  B *1:* 63

K

Karadzic, Radovan
  B *1:* 43
Karnow, Stanley
  A 137
Keating, Charles
  B *2:* 262
Kennedy, Caroline
  A 78 (ill.)
Kennedy, Edward
  A 78 (ill.), 242
Kennedy, Jacqueline Bouvier
  A 78 (ill.)
Kennedy, John F.
  A 51-52, 52 (ill.), 56, 58, 61,
    68, 71, 72, 73, 75, 76, 77,
    137, 138
  B *1:* 25-26, 27, 108, 151-52,
    165-73, 165 (ill.), 174, 175-
    77; *2:* 207-8, 238, 240, 267,
    274, 291, 293, 300, 326, 371,
    404, 408, 409
  PS 45
Kennedy, John F., and Cold War
  B *1:* 170-72, 173
Kennedy, John F., and 1960
  election
  B *1:* 47, 169-70
Kennedy, John F., assassination of
  B *1:* 172-73
Kennedy, John F., increases
  U.S. military aid to
  South Vietnam
  A 56

Kennedy, John F., Vietnam War
   policies of
   B *1:* 171-72, 173
Kennedy, John F., Jr.
   A 78 (ill.)
Kennedy, Robert F.
   A 78 (ill.), 114, 128, 129, 140,
   143-44
   B *1:* **174-80,** 174 (ill.);
   2: 267, 371
   PS 23, 49-54, 51 (ill.)
Kennedy, Robert F., antiwar
   speeches of
   PS 50-53
Kent State University shootings
   A 146-47, 147 (ill.), 200, 211
   B *2:* 328
   PS 24, 86, 92-93, 96, 98-111,
   99 (ill.)
Kent State University
   shootings, reaction of
   community to
   PS 101, 107-8
Kerrey, Bob
   PS 195
Kerry, John
   A 177, 193
   PS 195
Khe Sanh
   PS 123
Khe Sanh, Siege at
   A 115-17, 124, 125
   B *1:* 128
Khmer Rouge
   A 205, 206, 210, 253-54
   B *2:* 243, 245-48, 359-68, 389,
   392-94
Killing Fields, The
   B *2:* 362-63, 364, 365
Kim Phuc
   A 192 (ill.)
King, Coretta Scott
   A 207
King, Martin Luther, Jr.
   A 114, 129, 139 (ill.), 140, 142
   B *1:* 2, 9, 10-11, **181-88,**
   181 (ill.); *2:* 235
   PS 21-22, 25-42, 33 (ill.), 54
King, Martin Luther, Jr., and
   Vietnam War
   B *1:* 185-87
King, Martin Luther, Jr.,
   assassination of
   B *1:* 49

King, Martin Luther, Jr., Riverside
   Church speech
   B *1:* 186-87
Kissinger, Henry
   A 203, 226, 231, 234
   B *1:* **189-95,** 189 (ill.); *2:* 215,
   218, 219, 220-21, 221 (ill.),
   222, 255
Kit Carson Scouts
   PS 143
Kleberg, Richard
   B *1:* 149
Komer, Robert
   A 124
Korean War
   A 29
   B *2:* 408
Koster, Samuel
   B *1:* 33, 36
Kovic, Ron
   B *1:* **196-202,** 196 (ill.); *2:* 403
Krause, Allison
   PS 105, 106

L

Lam Son 719
   A 223
Landmines
   B *2:* 286
Lane, Sharon A.
   PS 176 (ill.)
Lansdale, Edward
   B *2:* **203-9,** 291
Laos
   A 50-51, 222-24, 223 (map),
   233, 254
   B *2:* 247, 340, 396-99
   PS 212-13
Laos, "Secret War" in *2:* 398
LaRouche, Lyndon
   B *1:* 42
Last Reflections on a War
   B *1:* 82-83, 86
Le Duan
   A 206, 244
   B *2:* **210-14,** 210 (ill.)
Le Duc Tho
   A 226, 230-31
   B *1:* 136, 189, 191, 192, 193;
   2: **215-23,** 215 (ill.), 221 (ill.)
Le Loi
   A 6

Le Ly Hayslip
   B *2:* **224-29,** 224 (ill.), 404-5
Le Thanh Tong
   A 6
Le Van Kim
   A 72
League for the Independence
      of Vietnam
   B *1:* 136
League of Wives of American
      Vietnam POWs
   PS 184
Lederer, William
   B *2:* 207
Lin, Maya
   A 283
   B *2:* **230-36,** 230 (ill.), 379
   PS 222 (ill.), 223-24, 231
Lodge, Henry Cabot, Jr.
   A 70 (ill.), 70-71, 72
   B *1:* 168; *2:* **237-42,**
      237 (ill.), 294
Lon Nol
   A 206, 210, 233
   B *2:* **243-48,** 243 (ill.), 362,
      366, 389, 392-93
Long-Haired Army
   B *2:* 314

M

MAAG-Vietnam. *See* Military
      Assistance Advisory
      Group-Vietnam
      (MAAG-Vietnam)
MACV. *See* Military
      Assistance Command-
      Vietnam (MACV)
Madame Nhu. *See* Ngo Dinh Nhu,
      Madame (Tran Le Xuan)
Magsaysay, Ramon
   B *2:* 204-5
Making of a Quagmire, The
   B *1:* 117
Malcolm X
   B *1:* 122
Mansfield, Mike
   A 89, 141
Mao Zedong
   A 27
March on the Pentagon
   A 140-41
   B *1:* 55-56, 94, 143-44

Martin, Graham
   A 250
   B *2:* **249-56,** 249 (ill.), 321
Maya Lin: A Strong, Clear Vision
   B *2:* 235
   PS 231
Mayaguez incident
   PS 227
McAlister, Elizabeth
   B *1:* 18
McCain, John
   B *2:* **257-64,** 257 (ill.), 260 (ill.)
   PS 181, 195
McCain, John S., Jr.
   B *2:* 257-58
McCain, John S., Sr.
   B *2:* 258
McCarran-Walter Act
   PS 218
McCarthy, Eugene
   A 128, 140, 143
   B *1:* 179
McCarthy, Joseph
   A 47
   B *1:* 107, 175-76
McGovern Family Foundation
   B *2:* 270
McGovern, George
   A 136, 148, 231
   B *1:* 5, 155; *2:* **265-71,**
      265 (ill.), 329
McNamara, Robert S.
   A 80, 80 (ill.), 87 (ill.), 94,
      107-11, 126
   PS 129, 144
McNamara, Robert S., doubts
      about U.S. ability to win
      Vietnam War
   A 107-10
   B *1:* 67; *2:* **272-80,** 272 (ill.),
      279 (ill.), 371, 410, 410 (ill.)
McNamara, Robert S., public
      expressions of confidence
      about U.S. war effort
   A 109
McNamara, Robert S., testimony
      before Senate subcommittee
   A 109
McNaughton, John
   B *1:* 66
Media coverage of Vietnam War
   PS 117-20, 121-23, 125-31
Medical exemptions
   PS 61-62

Medina, Ernest L.
   A 212, 213
   B *1:* 33
MIA (Missing in Action)
   controversy
   PS 192-95, 196
MIA soldiers. *See* Missing in
   Action (MIA) soldiers
Military Assistance Advisory
   Group-Vietnam
   (MAAG-Vietnam)
   A 43
Military Assistance
   Command-Vietnam (MACV)
   A 53
Military Revolutionary Council
   A 78-79
   B *2:* 318
Miller, Jeffrey
   PS 105, 106, 110
Milosevic, Slobodan
   B *1:* 43
Missing in Action (MIA) soldiers
   A 291
MOBE. *See* National Mobilization
   Committee to End the War
   in Vietnam (MOBE)
Montagnard tribespeople
   A 228-29, 229 (ill.)
Montgomery, G. V. "Sonny"
   PS 193
Moratorium Day demonstrations
   A 145, 207
   B *1:* 57, 146
Morrison, Norman R.
   B *2:* 276-77, 277 (ill.)
Morse, Wayne
   A 86
Muller, Bobby
   B *2:* **281-87**, 418
Muskie, Edmund
   B *1:* 3
My Lai massacre
   A 152, 170, 212-13, 214-15,
      214 (ill.)
   B *1:* 30, 32-36; *2:* 334
   PS 152-53, 163, 170-72, 174

N

Napalm
   A 95, 101, 125, 184, 192 (ill.),
      193, 196 (ill.)
   B *2:* 353-54

National Coordinating
   Committee to End the
   War in Vietnam
   A 138
National Council of
   Reconciliation
   B *1:* 192; *2:* 221
National Guard
National Guard, at Kent State
   University
   PS 98-111, 99 (ill.), 102 (ill.)
National Guard, military service in
   PS 62-63
National Leadership Committee
   B *2:* 305, 319
National League of Families of
   American Prisoners and
   Missing in Southeast Asia
   PS 192-93
National Liberation Front (NLF)
   A 50
   B *2:* 218, 292, 299, 311,
      313, 314
   PS 10
National Mobilization Committee
   to End the War in Vietnam
   (MOBE)
   B *1:* 52, 55
National Origins Act of 1924
   PS 218
National Union for Independence
   and Peace
   B *2:* 300
Nationalist movement,
   Vietnamese. *See* Vietnamese
   nationalist movement
NATO. *See* North Atlantic Treaty
   Organization (NATO)
Navarre, Henri
   A 32-33
Nelson, Gaylord
   A 191
Neuhaus, John
   B *1:* 19
New York Times
   B *2:* 384, 385
Newton, Huey
   B *1:* 122, 123, 123 (ill.)
Ngo Dinh Can
   A 42
   PS 44 (ill.)
Ngo Dinh Diem
   A 37, 39-43, 40 (ill.), 45, 51-54,
      61, 65-67, 68, 69, 78, 136

B *1:* 172; *2:* 203, 206-7, 208, 237, 239, **288-95**, 288 (ill.), 296, 297, 298, 300-301, 307, 313, 318, 346, 348, 411
PS 9, 44-46, 44 (ill.), 134
Ngo Dinh Diem, appointment of family members to key government posts
A 41
Ngo Dinh Diem, fall of
A 71-73
B *2:* 239, 240, 301-2
Ngo Dinh Diem, opposition to
A 48-52, 67, 69-70
Ngo Dinh Diem, persecution of political opponents
A 45-48, 67, 70
Ngo Dinh Diem, policies of
PS 44-45
Ngo Dinh Diem, U.S. concerns about
A 45, 51-52, 65-66
Ngo Dinh Khoi
B *2:* 289, 290
Ngo Dinh Luyen
PS 44 (ill.)
Ngo Dinh Nhu (Brother Nhu)
A 41-42, 57, 68-69, 70, 72-73
B *2:* 293, 294, 297, 298, 300-301, 301 (ill.)
PS 44 (ill.)
Ngo Dinh Nhu, Madame (Tran Le Xuan)
A 42, 69, 70, 73
B *2:* 293, 294, **296-302**, 296 (ill.)
PS 44 (ill.)
Ngo Dinh Thuc
A 42, 66
PS 44 (ill.)
Ngo Quyen
A 5
Ngo Vinh Long
A 16
Ngor, Haing S.
B *2:* 363, 363 (ill.)
PS 146
Nguyen Ai Quoc. *See* Ho Chi Minh
Nguyen Anh
A 7-8
Nguyen Cao Ky
A 110
B *2:* **303-10**, 303 (ill.), 319
PS 47

Nguyen Go Thach
B *2:* 280
Nguyen Hue
A 7
Nguyen Huu Co
B *2:* 305, 319
Nguyen Khanh
A 79-80, 88
B *2:* 305, 318
Nguyen Ngoc Loan
A 118, 119 (ill.)
Nguyen O Phap. *See* Ho Chi Minh
Nguyen That Than. *See* Ho Chi Minh
Nguyen Thi Binh
B *2:* 218-19, 219 (ill.)
Nguyen Thi Dinh
B *2:* **311-15**
Nguyen Van Am
PS 44 (ill.)
Nguyen Van Linh
A 268, 270-71
Nguyen Van Thieu
A 110, 204, 217-19, 224, 235, 237, 241-42, 245
B *1:* 192, 193; *2:* 219-21, 249, 250, 252, 305, 307, 309, **316-22**, 316 (ill.)
PS 48, 56-57, 81
Nguyen Van Thieu, and Paris Peace Accords
A 233
Nguyen Van Thieu, policies of
PS 48, 54-55
Nguyen Van Thieu, resignation of
A 248
Nhu, Madame. *See* Ngo Dinh Nhu, Madame (Tran Le Xuan)
Nickerson, Herman
PS 143
Night Flight to Hanoi
B *1:* 20
Nixon
B *2:* 404
Nixon, Richard M.
A 34, 82, 129, 148, 203 (ill.), 286
B *1:* 41, 103, 155, 200; *2:* 220, 238, 242, 249, 265, 268-69, 270, 320, **323-31**, 323 (ill.), 327 (ill.), 385, 404
PS 19, 22-23, 54, 63, 74, 77-94, 78 (ill.), 88 (ill.), 95

Nixon, Richard M., and antiwar
    movement
    A 144 (ill.), 207-9, 211, 225
Nixon, Richard M., and
    Cambodia
    A 205-6, 209-12
Nixon, Richard M., and feelings
    about antiwar movement
    PS 83-84
Nixon, Richard M., and invasion
    of Cambodia
    PS 95-96, 109
Nixon, Richard M., and Kent
    State University killings
    PS 109
Nixon, Richard M., and media
    coverage of Vietnam War
    PS 127, 128
Nixon, Richard M., and
    My Lai massacre
    A 213
Nixon, Richard M., and
    negotiations with
    North Vietnam
    A 200-203, 224, 226, 230-31,
    232-34
    B *1:* 191-94
Nixon, Richard M., and
    Pentagon Papers
    B *1:* 67-68, 71
Nixon, Richard M., and
    presidential election
    of 1972
    A 231
Nixon, Richard M., and
    presidential election
    of 1960
    B *1:* 47, 169-70
Nixon, Richard M., and
    presidential election
    of 1968
    A 130
    B *1:* 50
Nixon, Richard M., and
    Silent Majority
    A 145-46, 207-9
    PS 81
Nixon, Richard M., and
    Spiro Agnew
    B *1:* 2-5
Nixon, Richard M., and Vietnam
    policies
    A 199-215, 217, 222-35

Nixon, Richard M., and
    Vietnamization program
    A 145-46, 148
    B *2:* 323, 328
    PS 80, 81, 82, 89
Nixon, Richard M., and
    Watergate scandal
    A 149, 151, 226, 237, 239-41,
    240 (ill.)
Nixon, Richard M., and
    William Calley
    B *1:* 36
Nixon, Richard M., strategy
    in Laos
    A 222-24
NLF. *See* National Liberation
    Front (NLF)
Nobel Peace Prize
    B *2:* 215, 222, 287
Nolting, Frederick
    A 53, 65, 71
North Atlantic Treaty
    Organization (NATO)
    A 46
North Vietnam
    A 18, 20, 37, 39, 43-45, 49, 86
North Vietnam, land reform
    campaign of mid-1950s
    A 44
North Vietnam, 1975 invasion
    of South Vietnam by
    A 243-53
North Vietnam, 1973 invasion
    of South Vietnam by
    B *2:* 251-52
North Vietnam, victory over
    South Vietnam
    B *2:* 321
North Vietnamese Army (NVA)
    B *2:* 426
North Vietnamese Army (NVA),
    style of fighting
    A 100-101
Northern Lights
    B *2:* 335
Nurses in the U.S. military
    B *2:* 414
    PS 114, 165, 166-70, 167 (ill.),
    169 (ill.)
NVA. *See* North Vietnamese
    Army (NVA)

O

O'Brien, Tim
  A 167, 168, 169
  B *2:* 332-38, 332 (ill.)
  PS 23, 68-73, 69 (ill.)
Ochs, Phil
  B *1:* 10-11, 11 (ill.)
Ohio National Guard. *See*
  National Guard, at Kent State
"On the Rainy River"
  PS 68-73
Operation Babylift
  B *2:* 253
Operation Cedar Falls
  A 101
Operation Linebacker II. *See*
  Christmas Bombing
Operation Niagara
  A 125
Operation Rolling Thunder
  A 93-96, 94 (map)
  B *1:* 28, 158
Orderly Departure Program
  PS 206
OSS. *See* U.S. Office of Strategic
  Services (OSS)
Oswald, Lee Harvey
  A 76, 77
  B *1:* 172
Other Side, The
  B *1:* 124
Ottawa Treaty
  B *2:* 287

P

Pacification efforts
  A 116
Pacification programs
  B *2:* 241
*Page after Page: Memoirs of a
  War-Torn Photographer*
  B *2:* 344
Page, Tim
  B *2:* 339-45, 339 (ill.)
Palmer, Laura
  PS 226
Palo, Linda Phillips
  PS 226-30
Paris Peace Accords
  A 217-19, 232-33, 234, 239
  B *2:* 217-20, 221 (ill.)
  PS 55, 191

Path of Revolution in the South, The
  B *2:* 212
Pathet Lao
  A 50-51, 222, 254
  B *2:* 247, 397, 398, 399
  PS 212
PAVN. *See* People's Army of
  Vietnam (PAVN)
Peace and Freedom Party
  B *1:* 123
Peers, William R.
  A 212
  B *1:* 33
Pentagon Papers
  A 225-26
  B *1:* 64, 67-71; *2:* 382, 385
People's Army of
  Vietnam (PAVN)
  B *2:* 424
People's Coalition for Peace
  and Justice. *See* National
  Mobilization Committee
  to End the War in
  Vietnam (MOBE)
People's Revolutionary
  Government (PRG)
  B *2:* 218
Perot, H. Ross
  PS 188
Persian Gulf War
  A 287-89, (ill.)
  B *1:* 42
  PS 131
Pham Van Dong
  A 43, 203, 206
Pham Van Xinh
  A 247
Phan Boi Chau
  A 11
  B *1:* 136; *2:* 346-51, 346 (ill.)
Phan Chau Trinh
  B *2:* 218
Phan Dinh Khai. *See* Le Duc Tho
Phan Thi Kim Phuc
  B *2:* 352-58
Philippines
  B *2:* 204-5
Phnom Penh, fall of
  B *2:* 247
Phoenix Program
  A 116-17
Phuoc Hiep
  B *2:* 314

Phuoc Long
   A 244
Phuong Hoang
   PS 201-19
Platoon
   B *2:* 400, 402, 403
Pleiku
   B *2:* 415
Plummer, John
   B *2:* 357
Pol Pot
   A 254, 266, 271
   B *2:* 245, **359-68**, 359 (ill.), 392
Port Huron Manifesto
   B *1:* 121
Post-traumatic Stress
      Disorder (PTSD)
   A 182-83
   B *2:* 418, 419
   PS 176
Powell, Colin
   PS 176
POWs. *See* Prisoners of War,
      American
Presidential Design Award
   B *2:* 235
PRG. *See* People's Revolutionary
      Government (PRG)
Prisoners of War (POWs),
      American (POWs)
   A 93, 177, 181 (ill.), 232
   B *1:* 58, 59-62, 95-96; *2:* 221,
      257, 259-61
   PS 114-15, 179-96, 182 (ill.),
      187 (ill.)
Prisoners of War (POWs),
      American and antiwar
      movement
   PS 195-96
Prisoners of war (POWs),
      American, torture and
      mistreatment of
   B *1:* 160-62; *2:* 261
Prisoners of War (POWs), North
      Vietnamese
   PS 179-80, 183, 184 (ill.)
Profiles in Courage
   B *1:* 168
Project 100,000
   PS 26
Propaganda
   B *2:* 226

PTSD. *See* Post-Traumatic Stress
      Disorder (PTSD)
Pulitzer Prize
   B *2:* 354, 385, 387

Q

Quakers. *See* Society of Friends
Quang Duc
   A 67, 68 (ill.)
Quang Ngai Province
   B *2:* 334
Quang Tri City
   A 246
*Question of a National Liberation
   in Indochina, The*
   B *2:* 422
The Quiet American
   A 54, 55
   B *2:* 207

R

Racial tensions in the
      U.S. military
   PS 40-41
Rambo: First Blood, Part II
   PS 193
Ranariddh, Norodom
   B *2:* 394, 395
Ray, James Earl
   B *1:* 187
Rayburn, Sam
   B *1:* 149
Reagan, Ronald
   A 281 (ill.), 282, 285
   PS 194
Reeducation programs
   A 260-63
   PS 207
Refugee Assistance Act
   PS 218
Refugees. *See* Hmong People of
      Laos; Vietnamese refugees
Republic of Vietnam. *See* South
      Vietnam
*Requiem: By the Photographers
   Who Died in Vietnam*
   B *2:* 345
Reserve Officer Training Corps
      (ROTC) programs
   PS 101

Revolutionary Youth League
  B *2:* 211
Rhodes, James
  PS 98, 99, 103
Ridenhour, Ronald
  A 212
  B *1:* 33, 35-36
Risner, Robinson
  PS 181
Rockefeller Foundation
  B *2:* 371
Rockefeller, Nelson
  B *1:* 109
Roosevelt, Franklin D.
  A 19
Rostow, Walt
  A 56, 136
  B *2:* 409
ROTC programs. *See* Reserve
  Officer Training Corps
  programs (ROTC)
Royal Lao
  A 50
  B *2:* 397
Rubenstein, Bill
  PS 101, 103-6
Rubin, Jerry
  A 144
  B *1:* 144, 144 (ill.), 146
Ruby, Jack
  B *1:* 172
Rumor of War, A
  PS 114, 151, 153, 155, 156-61
Rusk, Dean
  A 136
  B *2:* 240, **369-74**, 369 (ill.)

S

Saigon
  A 194-96, 273 (ill.)
  B *2:* 254
Saigon, evacuation of
  A 249-52, 249 (ill.), 251 (ill.)
  B *2:* 252, 253-54, 255 (ill.)
Saigon, fall of
  A 248-53, 251 (ill.)
  B *2* 249, 252-55, 309
  PS 171, 172
Saigon Military Mission
  B *2:* 205-6

Saigon, North Vietnamese
    bombing of
  A 120 (ill.)
Saloth Sar. *See* Pol Pot
Satrom, Leroy
  PS 98
Schanberg, Sydney
  B *2:* 362, 364
SCLC. *See* Southern Christian
    Leadership Conference (SCLC)
Schlesinger, Arthur J.
  A 58
Schlesinger, James
  A 242
Schroeder, William
  PS 106, 110
Scott, Hugh
  A 212
Scranton, William
  B *2:* 241
  PS 103
Scruggs, Jan
  A 283
  B *2:* 232, 233, **375-81**, 375 (ill.)
  PS 221-23, 222 (ill.), 232 (ill.)
SDS. *See* Students for a
    Democratic Society (SDS)
Seale, Bobby
  A 144
  B *1:* 122-23, 123 (ill.)
Search and destroy missions
  A 97
  B *2:* 431
SEATO. *See* Southeast Asia Treaty
    Organization (SEATO)
Selective Service. *See* Draft, military
Sheehan, Neil
  A 65, 69, 137
  B *1:* 70; *2:* 308, **382-88**, 382 (ill.)
Sheuer, Sandy
  PS 105, 106, 109
Shrapnel in the Heart
  PS 226
Shriver, Sargent
  B *1:* 5; *2:* 270
Siege at Khe Sanh. *See* Khe Sanh,
    Siege at
Sihanouk, Norodom
  A 205-6
  B *2:* 243, 244-45, 246, 360, 362,
    363, 366, **389-95**, 389 (ill.)
Silent Majority
  A 145-46, 207-9
  PS 81

Sisowath Sirik Matak
 B *2:* 244, 245, 246, 392
Smith, Homer
 B *2:* 252
SNCC. *See* Student Nonviolent
  Coordinating Committee
  (SNCC)
Socialism
 A 44
Socialist Republic of
  Vietnam (SRV)
 A 257-76
 PS 197, 202
Socialist Republic of Vietnam
  (SRV), re-education of South
  Vietnamese citizens
 A 260-63
 B *2:* 213, 315, 346, 350
Society of Friends
 A 136
 PS 171
Soldier Reports, A
 B *2:* 436
Souphanouvong, Prince
 B *2:* 397, 399
South Vietnam
 A 37, 45, 75, 80
South Vietnam, dependence
  on U.S. military aid
 A 98
South Vietnam, economy of
 A 242
South Vietnam, government of
 PS 44-45, 48, 49, 52, 54-55,
  57, 123
South Vietnam, national
  elections
 A 110-11
South Vietnam Women's Union
  for Liberation
 B *2:* 218
South Vietnamese Army. *See*
  Army of the Republic of
  Vietnam (ARVN)
Southeast Asia Treaty
  Organization (SEATO)
 A 45
Southern Christian Leadership
  Conference (SCLC)
 B *1:* 183
Southern Poverty Law Center
 B *2:* 235
Souvanna Phouma
 B *2:* **396-99**, 396 (ill.)

Spellman, Francis
 B *1:* 19
Spock, Benjamin
 B *1:* 40, 40 (ill.)
Stockdale, James
 PS 115, 179, 185-86, 185 (ill.),
  186-90
Stockdale, Sybil
 PS 184, 188
Stone, Dana
 B *2:* 345
Stone, Oliver
 B *1:* 201, 202; *2:* 229, **400-405**,
  400 (ill.)
 PS 146
Strategic Hamlets Program
 A 57-59
Stratton, Richard
 PS 181
Street Without Joy
 B *1:* 81
Student deferments
 PS 61, 74
Student Nonviolent Coordinating
  Committee (SNCC)
 B *1:* 121
 PS 28
Students for a Democratic
  Society (SDS)
 A 139, 143, 144, 147
 B *1:* 119, 120-21, 125-26

T

Taylor, Maxwell D.
 A 56, 66, 73
 B *2:* 241, **406-12**, 406 (ill.),
  410 (ill.), 430
Teach-ins
 A 139
Ten Years After: Vietnam Today
 B *2:* 344
Tet Offensive
 A 111, 113, 118, 119-21,
  122-24, 143, 243
 B *1:* 28, 128, 161; *2:* 309, 342,
  426, 429, 433
 PS 48, 49, 50, 113, 120-21,
  122-23, 126-27, 128
Tet Offensive, effect on U.S.
  public's view of the war
 A 122-24

Tet Offensive, reassessment of
    U.S. war effort after
    A 126-27
They Call Us Dead Men
    B *1:* 20
Things They Carried, The
    B *2:* 332, 336-37
    PS 68
Thompson, Hugh C.
    A 212
    B *1:* 34-35
Tiger Cages
    PS 183
Tim Page's Nam
    B *2:* 343, 344
*To America with Love: Letters
    from the Underground*
    B *1:* 146
To Dwell in Peace
    B *1:* 22
Tonkin Gulf Resolution
    A 82, 84, 85-87, 213
    B *1:* 101-2, 158; *2:* 268
    PS 18
"Tragedy at Kent"
    PS 103-6
Tran Cong Man
    A 245
Tran Le Xuan. *See* Ngo Dinh Nhu,
    Madame (Tran Le Xuan)
Tran Van Chuong
    A 70
Tran Van Don
    A 45, 72
Tran Van Huong
    A 248
    B *2:* 252, 319
Trial
    B *1:* 125
Trial of the Catonsville Nine, The
    B *1:* 21
Truman, Harry S.
    A 19, 20, 27, 27 (ill.)
Truong Chinh
    B *2:* 213
Truong Son Route. *See* Ho Chi
    Minh Trail
Tu Duc
    A 8
Turner, Ted
    B *1:* 97
Twenty Years and Twenty Days
    B *2:* 306-7

*Two Viet-Nams: A Political and
    Military History*
    B *1:* 83

U

Ugly American, The
    B *2:* 207
Uncounted Enemy, The
    B *2:* 437
UNESCO. *See* United Nations
    Educational, Scientific, and
    Cultural Organization
    (UNESCO)
United Nations Educational,
    Scientific, and Cultural
    Organization (UNESCO)
    B *2:* 357
United Nations Food
    and Agriculture
    Organization (FAO)
    B *2:* 271
United Press International (UPI)
    B *2:* 340, 383
United States
United States, air bombing
    campaigns
    A 93, 227-30, 231-32, 233
United States, attitudes toward
    Vietnam veterans
    A 281-85
United States, bombing
    of Cambodia
    PS 82
United States, casualty figures
    A 110
United States, commitment of
    combat troops to Vietnam
    A 81, 87, 96, 138
United States, counterinsurgency
    techniques
    B *2:* 208
United States, diplomatic
    relations with Vietnam
    B *2:* 263
United States, early involvement
    in Vietnam
    A 37, 39, 45-48
    PS 9-11
United States, escalation of
    military involvement
    in Vietnam
    A 91

United States, foreign policy
   after Vietnam
   A 285-90
United States, frustration with
   Viet Cong
   PS 144-45
United States, internal debate
   over Vietnam War
   A 105-6, 108
United States, internal divisions
   over Vietnam War
   PS 79
United States, invasion of
   Cambodia
   B 2: 246, 328, 362
   PS 91-92
United States, military draft
   B 2: 333
United States, military
   performance in Vietnam
   A 219-22
United States, pacification efforts
   A 116
   B 2: 241
United States, postwar
   A 277-92
United States, postwar relations
   with Vietnam
   A 272, 290-92
   PS 195
United States, search and
   destroy missions
   A 97
   B 2: 431
United States, self-image
   after Vietnam
   A 278-80, 288-90
United States, strategy
   of attrition
   A 110
   B 2: 431
United States, treatment of
   returning veterans
   B 2: 416-17
United States, troop strength
   in Vietnam
   A 103
United States, views of
   Vietnamese refugees
   PS 204-5, 216-17
United States, withdrawal of
   troops from Vietnam
   B 2: 250

UPI. *See* United Press
   International (UPI)
U.S. Army Reserves, military
   service in
   PS 62-63
U.S. Central Intelligence
   Agency (CIA)
   A 40
   B 2: 203, 204, 205, 305
U.S. Congress, attitudes toward
   Vietnam War
   A 140-41, 211-14, 237, 239,
   242-43, 246, 247-48
   B 1: 101-3, 193-94
U.S. Declaration of Independence
   PS 6, 7
U.S. military, enlistment in
   PS 228
U.S. Office of Strategic
   Services (OSS)
   A 15
   B 2: 204
U.S. Veterans Administration
   A 182

V

Van Devanter, Lynda
   B 2: **413-20**, 413 (ill.)
Van Tien Dung
   A 230, 244, 250-51
   B 2: 222
Vang Pao
   PS 212
Vann, John Paul
   A 65
   B 1: 68-69; 2: 384, 385-87
*Vantage Point: Perspectives of the
   Presidency, 1963-1969, The*
   B 1: 157, 163
Vecchio, Mary
   PS 110
Veterans. *See* Vietnam veterans
Veterans Administration
   PS 177
Veterans of Foreign Wars (VFW)
   B 2: 379
VFW. *See* Veterans of Foreign
   Wars (VFW)
Viet Cong
   A 48-50, 54, 55, 57, 61, 62, 65,
   75, 79, 80, 86, 89, 100 (ill.),
   116-17

B *2:* 210, 213, 217-19, 224-27, 292, 299, 304-5, 311, 313, 314, 412, 425, 426
PS 10, 11, 134-35, 136-37, 138-44, 145, 170
Viet Cong, American frustration with
PS 144-45
Viet Cong, atrocities committed by
PS 151-53, 157-58
Viet Cong, decline in numbers after Tet Offensive
A 122
Viet Cong, style of fighting
A 100-101
B *2:* 431-32
Viet Cong, U.S. frustration with
A 100-101
Viet Minh
A 15, 17-18, 20, 23-24, 25, 29-31, 32, 33, 34, 38-39, 54, 55
B *1:* 136-38; *2:* 211, 216, 290, 312, 317, 347, 422, 423
PS 1, 5
Viet Nam Doc Lap Dong Minh (Vietnam Independence League). *See* Viet Minh
Vietnam
A 3 (map)
Vietnam, and *doi moi* reforms
A 268-70
Vietnam, diplomatic relations with United States
B *2:* 263
Vietnam, famine in
A 16-17
Vietnam, geography of
A 3
Vietnam, history of
A 1, 4-6, 7-9
Vietnam, 1979 invasion of Cambodia
A 258-59, 266-68, 270
B *2:* 247, 367, 393-94
Vietnam, postwar
A 257-76, 262 (ill.)
B *1:* 14
Vietnam, postwar relations with United States
A 272, 290-92
PS 195

Vietnam, under French colonialism
B *2:* 289
Vietnam Challenge
B *1:* 77-78
Vietnam Doc Lap Dong Minh Hoa. *See* Viet Minh
Vietnam Liberation Army
A 17
Vietnam veterans. *See also* American soldiers
A 175-86, 178 (ill.), 280-85, 290
B *2:* 283-86, 379, 416, 418
PS 199
Vietnam veterans, African American
A 185
Vietnam veterans, and antiwar movement
A 152-53, 179-80, 185
Vietnam veterans, antiwar
B *1:* 199-200
Vietnam veterans, disabilities among
PS 168
Vietnam veterans, feelings upon returning home
B *2:* 416-17
Vietnam veterans, medical care for
B *1:* 198-99, 200; *2:* 283
Vietnam veterans, popular culture treatments of
A 282, 284-85
Vietnam veterans, public attitudes toward
A 176-79, 185-86
B *1:* 199
PS 221
Vietnam veterans, return to Vietnam of
A 290
Vietnam veterans, treatment of
B *1:* 75
Vietnam veterans, women veterans
B *2:* 413, 416, 418, 419
Vietnam Veterans Against the War (VVAW)
A 152-53, 185
B *1:* 41, 200
Vietnam Veterans of America (VVA)
B *2:* 281, 284-85, 418

Vietnam Veterans of America
 Foundation (VVAF)
 B *2:* 281, 285, 286
Vietnam Veterans Memorial
 A 194, 280 (ill.), 283-84, 284 (ill.)
 B *1:* 75; *2:* 230, 231, 232-34,
 285, 352, 356, 375, 378, 379,
 380-81
 PS 199, 221-26, 228, 229-33,
 231 (ill.), 232 (ill.)
Vietnam Veterans Memorial
 Fund (VVMF)
 B *2:* 232, 233, 234, 375,
 378, 381
 PS 221, 223
Vietnam Veterans of America
 Women's Project
 B *2:* 413, 419
 PS 176
Vietnam War
Vietnam War, battle sites
 A 243 (map)
Vietnam War, creation
 of refugees
 A 103
Vietnam War, effect
 on Cambodia
 B *2:* 245, 246, 361-62, 366,
 391, 392
Vietnam War, effect on Laos
 B *2:* 398-99
Vietnam War, effect on South
 Vietnamese land
 PS 170, 173
Vietnam War, effect on South
 Vietnamese people
 A 101-3
 B *1:* 89; *2:* 226
 PS 47-48, 49, 52, 55, 57,
 113-14, 133, 134-37,
 138-44, 170, 173
Vietnam War, effect on
 U.S. economy
 A 104-5
Vietnam War, impact on
 Vietnamese land
 A 102 (ill.), 188-91, 228
Vietnam War, impact on
 Vietnamese people
 A 187-98
Vietnam War, media coverage of
 A 53-56, 118-19
 B *1:* 113, 114-17; *2:* 384
 PS 117-20, 121-23, 125-31

Vietnam War, nurses and relief
 workers in
 PS 114, 165, 166-70, 167 (ill.),
 169 (ill.)
Vietnam War, U.S. debate over
Viet-Nam Witness, 1953-1966
 B *1:* 83
Vietnam Women's Memorial
 B *1:* 73, 75-77
Vietnamese Communist Party
 B *2:* 315, 422
 A 105-6, 108
Vietnamese Declaration
 of Independence
 PS 6-7
Vietnamese land, war's impact on
 A 102 (ill.), 188-91, 228
Vietnamese nationalist
 movement
 A 12-14, 15-16
Vietnamese people, war's
 impact on
 A 187-98, 221 (ill.)
 B *1:* 89
Vietnamese refugees
 A 191-94, 258, 264-66, 265 (ill.)
 B *1:* 14; *2:* 214
 PS 197-98, 201-6, 205 (ill.),
 214 (ill.)
Vietnamese Revolutionary
 Youth League
 B *1:* 136
Vietnamese Women's
 Solidarity Movement
 B *2:* 298
Vietnamese Workers' Party
 B *2:* 210, 212
Vietnamization
 A 145-46, 199, 203-4, 217
 B *2:* 323, 328, 434
 PS 54, 55, 80, 81, 82, 89, 95
VIVA. *See* Voices in Vital America
Vo Nguyen Giap
 A 31, 31 (ill.), 118, 125,
 206, 230
 B *2:* 279, 280, 346, **421-28,**
 421 (ill.), 432
Voices in Vital America (VIVA)
 PS 193
Volunteering for military service
 PS 68
VVA. *See* Vietnam Veterans of
 America (VVA)

VVAF. *See* Vietnam Veterans of
America Foundation (VVAF)
VVAW. *See* Vietnam Veterans
Against the War (VVAW)
VVMF. *See* Vietnam Veterans
Memorial Fund (VVMF)

W

Wallace, George
A 129
War crimes. *See* Atrocities
War Powers Act
A 239
B *2:* 329
War Powers Resolution
A 149
War Resisters League (WRL)
A 136, 138
Warren, Earl
A 77
B *1:* 172
Watergate scandal
A 149, 225-26, 237, 239-41
B *1:* 5; *2:* 323, 329-30
Welsh, Anne Morrison
B *2:* 277
Westmoreland, William C.
A 73, 96, 97, 104, 111, 115-16,
117-18, 125, 126, 128
B *2:* **429-35**, 429 (ill.)
Wheeler, Jack
B *2:* 378
*When Heaven and Earth Changed
Places: A Vietnamese Woman's
Journey from War to Peace*
B *2:* 224, 228
PS 114, 137-44
When Hell Was in Session
B *1:* 58, 61, 62
White, Robert
PS 106
Whiz Kids
B *2:* 273
Williams, Jody
B *2:* 286, 287

Winter Soldier Investigation
A 152-53
Women, in the U.S. military
PS 165, 177
Women, reporters in Vietnam
PS 166
Women veterans
B *2:* 413, 416, 418, 419
PS 175-76
Women veterans, U.S.
government treatment of
PS 176
Workers World Party
B *1:* 43
World Bank
B *2:* 278
World War II
A 14
B *2:* 407-8
WRL. *See* War Resisters
League (WRL)

X

Xam Ap Lo. *See* Briarpatch, the
Xuan Loc
A 248
Xuan Thuy
B *2:* 217

Y

Yippies. *See* Youth International
Party
Young Turks
B *2:* 305, 318
Youth International Party
B *1:* 141

Z

Zinn, Howard
B *1:* 20
Zoo, the
PS 181

Harris County Public Library
Houston, Texas